Build A Pole Woodshed

By Mary Twitchell

More and more people are turning to wood as a primary or second-ary heating fuel, and as this number increases, so too does the sophistication of our wood stoves/furnaces, and our knowledge of wood heat. By late autumn there are few homesteads, particularly in the northern rural areas, which aren't obscured by their seeming-ly infinite cords of split wood — cords stacked outside or in sheds to *season*. Properly seasoned wood is as important a part of the woodburning process as a well-constructed stove or a safe installa-tion.

Most woodburners now know that green wood can be as much as 65 percent water. This means that in burning a piece of green wood, as much as 1200 BTU's per pound (or 1/8 the potential heat value of the log), is lost in evaporating the moisture. In addition, wet wood is much more difficult to ignite and to keep burning. Worst of all, it produces more creosote which creates a potential fire hazard.

Wood Must Dry

Getting the full heat value from a piece of wood is very simple. The wood must be allowed to dry, and preferably for two years. (Seasoning times vary with the climate; in the desert wood dries much more quickly, in colder wetter areas drying may take two years or more.)

Over this two-year period, the green wood dries at various rates. Much of the moisture evaporates very quickly. In the first three months the seasoning is half complete and the fuel value is 90 percent of what it will be when thoroughly dried (evaporation also depends on temperature and humidity). In the next six to nine months, the wood is reasonably dry; in two years it will be as dry as it will get.

If you have invested time, energy, and money in a wood stove installation, it's foolish to forego a further savings by burning green wood. It requires *no* work to let wood season, and in the process you are increasing its heat value; the wood will be lighter, ignite better, and produce less smoke and fewer sparks.

The following pages outline various ways to speed the seasoning process — from no-cost methods of stacking the wood properly to building a low-cost, pole-built storage shed.

Preparing Wood for Storage

After a tree is felled, it should be bucked to length, then split. Splitting is easiest when the wood is green and preferably frozen. Wood can be left round if under six inches in diameter. If the logs are of greater diameter, they should be split to prevent decay and accelerate the drying process. Since wood dries more rapidly along the grain, it is necessary to break the water barrier — the bark — to let this process occur. Splitting also increases the surface area which speeds up drying.

It is essential to split birch and alder or they will rot. Don't be shy about splitting wood; you can always use kindling. In addition, splitting reduces the sizes to be burned, and wood stoves/furnaces burn cleaner and more efficiently if fed splits of no more than six inches in diameter.

Open-Air Stacking

Indoor or basement storage may seem the most logical way to dry wood, but you will probably have to contend with dirt and insects. There will be fewer problems if the wood is stored outdoors with a week's supply stacked in the basement or on an enclosed porch for easy access.

Wood piled outdoors against an exterior wall of the house is conveniently located, and you won't have to negotiate cellar stairs with armloads of wood. It also keeps the dirt and insects outside, but the exterior house walls will cut down on air circulation to the pile, water may drain off the house onto it, and it may dry very slowly, if at all.

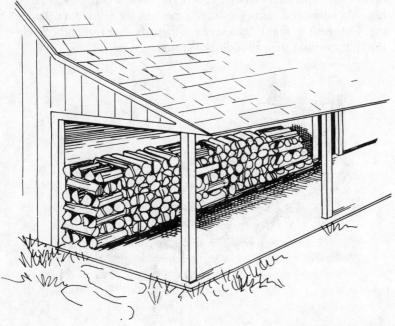

Wood stacked on a porch for seasoning.

If you have a concrete patio, wood can be piled there. Otherwise, locate the pile within a reasonable distance of the house. If the pile is located too far away, getting to it will be difficult in winter; if located too close, insects may be a problem, fire a hazard, and good air circulation more difficult to achieve.

Avoid damp places or depressions where water will collect after a rainfall or during the spring runoff. Loose soils dry the fastest; clayey soils the slowest. The wood should have maximum exposure to the sun and wind. The best location is on a hilltop or knoll where there are more air currents.

Consider the prevailing winds. The longer dimension of the pile should be exposed to the summer winds.

Lay down two stringers (poles of three to four inches in diameter) running the length of the pile. Anything can be improvised for support (stones, 2 × 4s, metal pipes) as long as it raises the pile about four inches off the ground to prevent decay and rot. Place the stringers a foot or so apart, and leave plenty of space between the piles.

The stringers can be of any length, but if you're curious about the number of cords of wood that you've cut, they should be eight feet long. At either end, drive in stakes to prevent the pile from collapsing. Cut them so that when driven in they are four feet high. Stack the splits so that they straddle the stringers.

Stacking wood on stringers speeds curing.

It is a real annoyance to have a pile tip over in the middle of winter. As a precaution, pile the last two splits in every row crosswise and tilt them slightly towards the pile to give it more stability.

The splits will air-dry more quickly if, after the first layer, the entire next layer is laid criss-cross, and the direction of the splits alternated with each tier until the pile starts to wobble. Leave the splits stacked criss-cross for three months, then restack them in the normal, parallel fashion.

Wood without bark will dry faster, but stripping it is impractical. Strip elm of bark to prevent the further spread of Dutch elm disease. This bark should be burned or the beetle will continue its nefarious activities once the weather warms.

If wood is totally exposed to the elements to air-dry, the moisture content of the wood may vary considerably with the season and the humidity. In some areas wood will dry rapidly in May and June; reabsorb water in July and August; dry out again in September; reabsorb in October.

The pile will be somewhat protected if the top layer of splits is turned bark-side-up. The bark will help shed rain. Even better is to cover the top of the pile with clear plastic sheeting, a tarp, pieces of tin, or any non-porous covering which will protect the wood from the worst of the weather.

Solar Dryer

A more permanent solution and one which will hasten drying is to build a solar dryer.

Four poles, two of which are one foot taller than the pile and two which are three feet taller, should be driven in six to twelve inches beyond each of the four corners with the shorter poles on the windward side. Then cover the pile with 4-mil clear polyethylene. The plastic should be stapled to the poles to form a shed-like structure, with a vent at the top of the high side. Don't let the plastic touch the pile and don't let it go all the way to the ground on any of the sides because air must be able to pass from the bottom of the pile through the splits and out the top vent. If there is no way for the air to escape, the water vapor which is released from the wood will condense on the surface of the plastic, and later be reabsorbed by the wood.

In sunny weather, the temperatures within the dryer will rise much higher than the outside temperatures. This heat will eliminate beetle and insect problems, while producing air-dried wood in three months.

The disadvantage of a solar dryer is that the intensity of the summer sun will deteriorate the plastic. Consequently this method is best for spring, fall, and winter protection. During the summer, the pile may have to be re-roofed.

Attached Woodshed

Some homes can be adapted for an attached wood storage facility, or it can be designed into houses under construction. Attached sheds with a pass-through door allow easy access from the house, and you won't have to don winter clothes to bring in the wood. Every week the shed may have to be reloaded or the wood rearranged. Be sure the door fits tightly.

For convenience, have a woodshed close to the house, and a door through which wood can be loaded into an inside wood box.

Wood Storage Shed

Open-air drying reduces the moisture in wood 14-25 percent; a woodshed will reduce it another 10-15 percent; indoor drying will add another 5-15 percent. For best results wood should be dried one year outdoors, then one year in a woodshed, with a week's supply dried indoors just before it is used. This means that to solve the problems of storing and seasoning wood, the serious woodburner should think about building a permanent, free-standing woodshed. The shed keeps insects and dirt to a minimum, while allowing the wood to dry under ideal conditions.

Location

The best location for your woodpile is also perfect for your storage shed. Since the wood will probably spend a year drying in the open air and then be moved into the shed, the piles should be located close to one another. The wood for burning will come from the shed, so it should be situated closer to the house. A short trip from shed to house will be appreciated all winter.

In choosing the location of the shed, consider water runoff and the soil composition. Loose soil dries fastest and makes a solid base for the foundation posts. The shed should be oriented with maximum exposure to the sun and wind. In cold regions the long dimension should run north/south to get the most heat from the morning and afternoon sun. If possible, the longer and most exposed side should be open to the summer winds, with the least exposure to blustery winter winds which will fill the shed with rain and snow. (Consider the location of buildings, trees, hills, or other barriers which might offer protection.) Usually the shed should face south or southwest. If the north side is unprotected, trees might be planted, or the north side of the shed enclosed.

Siting the shed will depend on the prevailing winds and the many variables of a location.

Preliminaries

Pole construction is one of the cheapest, easiest, and most appropriate ways to build a storage shed. The only excavation required is digging holes for the poles. No foundation or slab is necessary; since wood piles have to be raised anyway for ventilation, it would needlessly add to the expense. Pole buildings are suspended between load-bearing members which are embedded in the ground. Therefore load-bearing walls can be omitted without structural weakness. This cuts down on the amount of lumber that would be used if the shed were built using conventional construction techniques.

Pole buildings can be erected rapidly because the construction is simple. Very little carpentry skill is required. Two people will be needed to set and plumb the posts; the rest of the work can be done by any unskilled worker. These buildings are easy to construct; simple to maintain — and cheap.

The initial cost of a pole building is low, and can be even lower if you scrounge some of the materials. You may be able to buy used utility poles from the telephone company. Metal roofing may be salvaged from a barn or house which is being re-roofed.

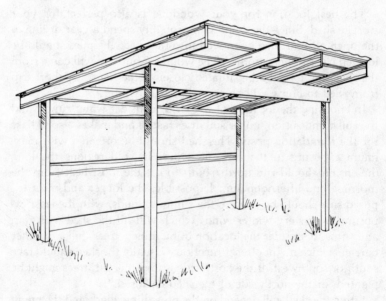

Pole wood storage shed.

Posts

The corner posts can be poles of at least six inches in diameter at their tips or 4 × 4s spaced at eight-foot intervals and sunk to below the frost line. Since these posts serve as the structural framework, it is essential that they be protected from decay. Wood deteriorates because of insects, dampness, bacteria, and fungi. To retard this process, wood can be sprayed with a fungicide and then pressure-impregnated with a preservative. You may prefer to creosote the wood yourself. However the creosote will not penetrate as far into the wood as pressure treatment and the wood will rot eventually. Cedar and hemlock are more naturally rot-resistant than other woods but still lack the longevity of those which have been pressure-impregnated. The pressure-treated poles of the telephone company will last forty to fifty years.

Size

The size of your shed will depend on your wood heating needs and the methods you intend to use for drying your wood supply. Since wood is cheaper to buy green, you should be buying your wood a year in advance of when you will be burning it. This means that, ideally, you will need storage space for at least one year's supply (if you plan to air-dry the wood for one year before moving it into the shed). If you don't want to move the wood, the shed should be large enough to store a two years' supply.

A homestead heated solely with wood will require seven to ten cords per year. Smaller homes which are tight and well-insulated may burn only two to three cords a year.

Wood Measurements

Wood is measured by divisions of a *standard cord*, which is a neatly stacked pile eight feet long by four feet wide by four feet high covering 128 cubic feet. Only 60-110 cubic feet of the 128 may be solid wood because wood cannot be stacked without air space. (Usually a cord runs between eighty to ninety cubic feet with more solid wood content in round wood than split.) Few people have four-foot fireplaces and many lack the equipment to reduce four-

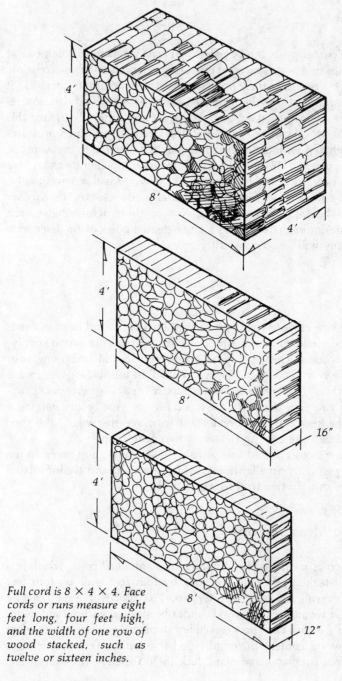

4'

8'

4'

4'

8'

16"

4'

8'

12"

Full cord is 8 × 4 × 4. Face
cords or runs measure eight
feet long, four feet high,
and the width of one row of
wood stacked, such as
twelve or sixteen inches.

foot lengths to stove dimension. Therefore wood sold in face cords, or lengths corresponding to either fireplace dimension (twenty inches) or stove dimension (twelve to sixteen inches), is more common. A *face cord* is a pile neatly stacked eight feet long by four feet high by whatever dimension you specify. A *rick* usually refers to sixteen-inch lengths.

A *run* is also a face cord, and varies in size depending on wood length. For example, wood cut to twenty-four-inch lengths means there are two runs in a cord; cut to sixteen-inch lengths, three runs to the cord; cut to twelve-inch lengths, four runs to the cord. To complicate matters further, there is a *unit* which is 1/24 of a standard cord, or a pile two feet by sixteen inches by two feet — the amount of wood which will fit into a station wagon or car trunk.

These measurements are important particularly if you are buying wood and want to be sure you have received what you paid for. They also will help you gauge how much firewood you will need for the heating season.

How Much Wood?

Can you figure out how much wood you will need to heat your home if you haven't used a wood stove before?

The University of Wisconsin Extension Service in its publication, *Wood for Home Heating,* suggests this method. "The easiest way to figure how much fuel wood you will need for a heating season is to convert your present fuel consumption to wood equivalents.

"Below are figures to help convert your present fuel to wood equivalents. A standard cord of wood is a stack 4' × 4' × 8'; it includes 80 cubic feet of solid wood. The heavier (better) hardwoods weigh, per standard cord, between 3,000 to 4,000 pounds when air-dry, so you can use an average of 3,500 pounds per cord for your estimate.

"1 gallon of #2 fuel oil = 22.2 pounds of wood
"1 therm (100 cubic feet) of natural gas = 14 pounds of wood
"1 gallon of propane gas = 14.6 pounds of wood
"1 kilowatt-hour of electricity = 0.59 pounds of wood
"1 pound of coal = 1.56 pounds of wood.

"Using #2 fuel oil as an example, if you burn 1,000 gallons of fuel oil, then 1,000 × 22.2 = 22,200 pounds of wood. Dividing 22,200 by 3,500 means you would need 6 1/3 standard cords of wood."

Gauge your firewood needs for the coming winter by using your last year's heating fuel requirement. Convert this number into cords and double it if you plan to store a two years' supply of wood in the storage shed.

But doubling the storage space will means you're building quite a large woodshed. If your requirements were ten cords a year, for example, you would need a woodshed that measured 8 × 8 × 40 for a total of 2560 cubic feet. A two-year supply for three cords per year would call for a woodshed 8 × 8 × 12.

There's another approach, to cut the size of the woodshed required. Plan to store the wood supply for the following winter in the woodshed, and the supply cut for the next year after that under plastic for a year. The only disadvantage of this is that you will have to move the wood from the plastic covering to the woodshed.

The 8 × 8 × 8 structure is very practical, holding four cords. If your demand for a woodshed is less than this, hold to this minimum size rather than not making full use of the pole design.

Big Enough

When deciding on the size of your woodshed, build large enough so that your wood supply can be stored easily. For example, if reaching high with wood is impossible for you, plan your woodshed so your supply can be contained if your pile is no more than six feet high.

Building instructions here are for the 8 × 8 × 8-foot module. For more space, the shed easily can be made to an 8 × 8 × 16-foot or 8 × 8 × 24-foot size. For more space, increase the length, while keeping the eight-foot height and width. If the shed is made any higher, stacking the wood becomes a problem; if the shed is wider, air will not circulate through it as well.

Materials

Lumber

amt.	dimension	use
2	4′ × 4′ × 12′ (Pressure-treated)	corner posts (front)
2	4′ × 4′ × 10′ (Pressure-treated)	corner posts (back)

(Poles can be substituted for the posts; they should be of the same heights, and approximately six inches thick at the tips. Be sure they have been pressure-treated. See *Pole Depth* for possible need for longer poles.)

amt.	dimension	use
4	2″ × 6″ × 12′	rafters
2	2″ × 8″ × 8′	girders
7	2″ × 4″ × 8′	purlins
1	2″ × 4″ × 12′	batter boards (can be scrap lumber)
4	1″ × 6″ × 10′	batter boards (can be scrap lumber)

Scrap lumber (1″ × 2″ or furring strips)

Hardware

1 1/2 lbs. 10d nails   1/2 lb. 16d nails

Tools

Tape measure
Mason's cord
2 8-foot ladders
Plumb bob
Chalkline
Hammer
4′ or 2′ carpenter's level

Handsaw
Line level
Post hole digger
Crowbar (may not be necessary)
Hand shovel
Combination square

The Construction Process

Site Preparation

Drive in stakes eight feet apart with a nail in the top of each to roughly mark the corners of the shed. Consider the terrain enclosed by this area. An excessive slope may necessitate some grading; a natural depression which will fill with rain or snow runoff may need to be leveled. Avoid these conditions, if possible.

Once the approximate corners have been established, check whether the area is square by measuring the diagonals — the lines between opposite stakes. Adjust the stakes until the diagonals are of the same length.

Outside the stakes at each of the four corners, erect *batter boards*. Drive three 2 × 4 stakes into the ground, spaced four to five feet apart, and to these nail 1″ × 6″ × 5′ boards so they form a right angle. These boards should be about ten to eighteen inches above the ground.

Square It

Level strings should be stretched taut between the boards; where they intersect should mark the outside corners of the building. Drop a plumb bob from the intersection of the two strings to the nail head to establish the precise corners. The strings will probably need adjustment.

Another way to check for squareness is to use the 3-4-5 principle (Pythagorean theorem). Measure from one corner three feet along one edge and mark this point with a stake. From this same corner, measure along the other leg of the right angle four feet and mark it. The distance between these two points should be five feet. Again, adjustments may be made to insure you have squared up the shed corners. Any multiple of these numbers can be used; if you are building a larger shed, 6-8-10 may be more accurate since it means you are checking the angle of a corner over a longer distance.

Cut a notch a saw kerf in width at precisely the place where the string is located on each of the batter boards. This allows you to remove the strings while the holes are being dug yet to replace them whenever you want to check the alignment of the holes.

Check the strings for level. Rest a four-foot carpenter's level on the string, or use a line level. The saw kerf may need to be adjusted so that all strings will read level.

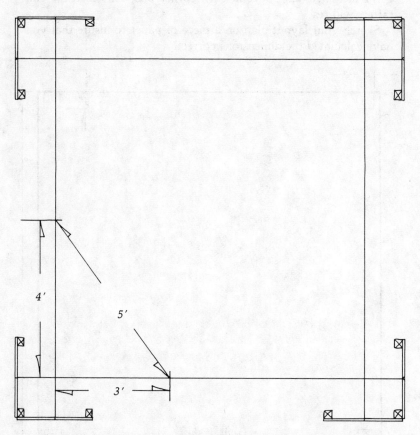

Batter boards and strings are used for locating the four corners of the shed. To check for squareness, measure from one corner three feet along one edge. Measure four feet along the other leg of the right angle. The distance between these two points should be five feet, if the corner is a true right angle.

Pole Spacing

It is most convenient to space the poles so that dimension lumber can be used. The strings mark the *outer* perimeter of the shed. The *center* of the post holes should be marked before digging, and these points will depend on whether you will be using round poles or 4 × 4 s. This "center" point should be adjusted further to allow for the girders. Move the corner posts towards the center of the shed an extra 1 1/2 inches (see illustration). This allows the girders a 1 1/2-inch overhang beyond each corner post on which the end rafters will rest.

Sketch your layout plan on a piece of paper to insure that you have calculated the dimensions correctly.

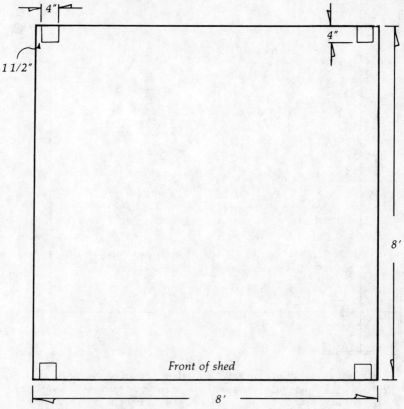

Pole spacing. Moving poles in from corner as shown permits placement of girders with slight overhang, where rafters will rest.

Pole Depth

As a rule 4″ × 4″ posts should be sunk 4′4″ in poor soil; 3′6″ in average soil; and 2′8″ in good soil. If your soil is loose or sandy, the posts will be more secure set in concrete. Generally, posts sunk three feet should be secure enough if the soil is relatively stable, and earth or gravel is tamped around the base.

Remove the strings. With a post hole digger, dig the holes. A shovel will disturb the earth too much. For posts which will be tamped with earth or gravel, make the hole twice the post's diameter. Angle the digger so that the hole widens towards its bottom if the post will be set in concrete. Add another six inches to the depth of the hole for gravel. This will provide drainage and prevent the butt of the pole from sitting in a puddle of water.

Gasoline-powered augers can be rented and should be used by those with bad backs or by those with more holes to dig than they can handle. Periodically the bit will have to be raised and cleaned of dirt. If you hit a rock, stop the motor and remove the auger. A crowbar or pick will have to be used to pry the rock loose.

Setting and Aligning the Posts

Setting and aligning the posts is the most important step in constructing a shed because the weight of the structure is borne by these posts. You will need a helper or two.

Drop a couple shovelfuls of gravel in the hole. On top of this, place a flat rock on which the pole will rest. Begin with the two 10-footers of the rear of the shed. They will be lighter to handle. With two or three people, lift the pole hand over hand into an upright position. Try to disturb as little soil as possible. A 1″ × 4″ placed under the butt of the pole may help in allowing you to lift against the board rather than against the edge of the hole.

Once the pole is in place, drive two stakes on adjacent sides of it, on the north and east sides, for example. To these nail a 1″ × 2″ which will be long enough to span a diagonal from the stake to the post.

Before bracing a pole, check carefully so that it is turned with the squarest side of the pole facing the eave. This will make it easier when nailing in the rafter.

Rest a 2- or 4-foot carpenter's level against the post and plumb

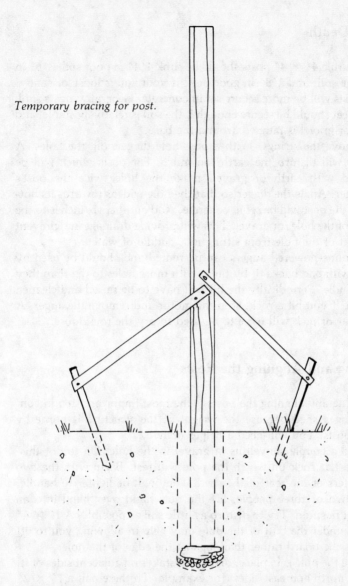

Temporary bracing for post.

the side adjacent to the 1 × 2 bracing. When this side is plumb have your helper nail the 1 × 2 to the post. Plumb the side adjacent to the second brace; nail the 1 × 2.

After both 10-footers are braced, replace the perimeter string. Measure from the string to the top of the posts. This distance should be the same on both poles.

You can adjust for uneven ground by changing the depth of the hole; add or remove gravel to make minor adjustments in height. Larger adjustments can be made by digging a deeper hole. Poles can even be cut later to the right height with a chain saw but this involves dangerous cutting from a ladder.

Erect the twelve-foot posts, align, plumb, and brace them. Check them for height. Then if the structure is larger than an 8' × 8' × 8' shed, erect the intermediate posts. Plumb these posts by stretching two strings between the end posts — one six to twelve inches from the ground, the second near the top of the posts. Intermediate posts should align with these strings. Have a helper sight along the strings to assure the posts are plumb.

Securing the Posts

One person should be constantly checking the posts for plumb, while a second person secures the posts in place. Shovel a layer of dirt into the hole and tamp it down with a hoe or the head of a crowbar. Add a second layer and continue the process. Near the top of the hole, use the heel of your boot to pack the earth as tightly as possible. At the top of the hole, shape a conical earth mound around the hole. Tamp this down and add more dirt if necessary so that there will be a cone left around each post. You want to insure there will still be a mound to divert runoff water from entering the hole.

If you intend to set the posts in concrete, use a concrete mix of one part cement, three parts sand, five parts gravel. Put the pole in place, then fill the hole, leaving a slight mound at the top which should be beveled towards the edges to lead runoff water away from the pole. The post should be checked for plumb and adjusted, if necessary, while the concrete is drying. Wait twenty-four hours before removing the braces.

Frame Construction

Two girders of 2" × 8" × 8' are nailed to the front and back of the shed to support the rafters. If you've calculated correctly, the girders should overhang 1 1/2 inches on each end. This gives the rafters something to sit on.

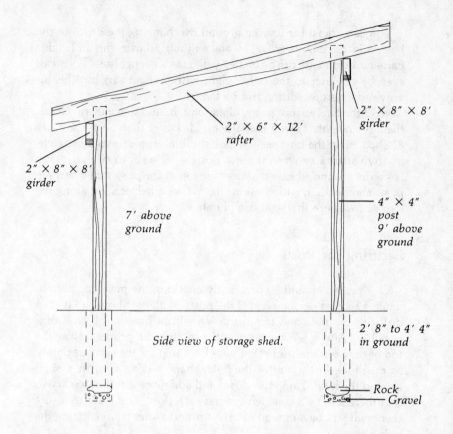

2" × 6" × 12' rafter

2" × 8" × 8' girder

2" × 8" × 8' girder

4" × 4" post 9' above ground

7' above ground

Side view of storage shed.

2' 8" to 4' 4" in ground

Rock
Gravel

You will need two 8-foot ladders and a helper for nailing the girders in place. Nail them so that the top edge of the 2" × 6" × 12' rafters will clear the posts. Otherwise the posts will interfere with the roof.

If the poles are at slightly different heights, you can adjust now. Hold one end of the girder about five inches down on the taller post. Drive in a 16d nail part way. With a helper holding the other end of the girder, move your ladder to the center of the girder and with a two- or four-foot level, adjust the girder until it reads level. If this leaves enough space on the posts to nail the end rafters, the girder can be nailed in place permanently. Use five 16d nails for each post. To lessen the chances of splitting, stagger the nails so that they aren't entering the same grain in the wood.

For sheds larger than 8' × 8', the girders should have 1 1/2-inch overhang at each end, but be butted where they meet at intermediate posts. You may have to square the ends of the girders to make a better butt joint.

Rafters

There will be four 2" × 6" × 12' rafters for an 8' × 8' shed. For each additional eight-foot section, three more rafters will be needed.

See the illustration on spacing the rafters. Note that the spacing between the two on the left is 30 1/2 inches, while the space between the second and third and third and fourth is 32 inches.

Facing the front of the shed, begin at the left end of the front girder, and measure in 30 1/2 inches, mark and square off this point with a combination square. Put an "X" to the right of the line. Continue this pattern down the girder, measuring for the next two in thirty-two-inch increments.

Do exactly the same on the rear girder, remembering to work from left to right and to make the "X" to the right of the line. Put one of the end rafters in place, leaving a 1 1/2-foot overhang on the lower eave. This rafter should rest on the 2" × 8" girders. Nail the end rafters into the posts or toe-nail them into the girders with three 10d nails.

The intermediate rafters should be nailed in place. Toe-nail them with two or three 10d nails, at least one on each side.

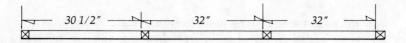

Shed Roof

Conventional roofs are sheathed with plywood or tongue-and-groove boards, over which felt paper is stapled, then roll roofing or asphalt shingles are laid. Metal roofing can be put down on top of decking and felt paper. However, there are metal roofs which are even easier and cheaper to install. Purlins are nailed at right angles to the rafters twenty-four inches on center and to these the metal roofing is nailed. This saves time and materials.

Metal roofs are lightweight, fire resistant, and under normal conditions will last longer than a conventional roof. Installation is simple, and for a shed or garage where heat retention is of no concern, metal roofs are more than adequate.

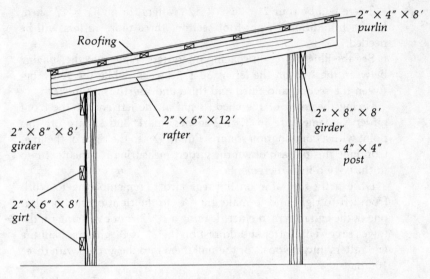

Roofing

2" × 4" × 8' purlin

2" × 6" × 12' rafter

2" × 8" × 8' girder

4" × 4" post

2" × 8" × 8' girder

2" × 6" × 8' girt

Roofing details of shed.

Purlins

In order to have something to support the metal roofing, 2" × 4" purlins are added on top of and perpendicular to the roof rafters. Place these on twenty-four-inch centers. Beginning from the lower eave, measure twenty-four inches. Use a combination square to mark the location, draw an "X." From this line measure 24 inches, draw a line, then the "X." Do likewise on the opposite side of the shed, being sure the "Xs" fall to the same side of the line. (Before placing the purlins, check the roof manufacturer's instructions. Spacing varies from sixteen inches to twenty-two inches with different metal roofs.)

You will find it easier to nail the purlins with a helper. With one eight-foot ladder at either end of the shed, line up the first purlin with the rafter tails. Nail it in place with two 10d nails at each rafter. Stagger the nails so that they don't enter the same grain of the wood.

Place the next purlin in place. To be sure you have made your "Xs" to the same side of the line, check the distance *between* the rafters. (It should be 20 1/2 inches) Continue with all seven purlins.

Types of Metal Roofing

Flat and ridged metal roofs are laid with locked or soldered joints. These roofs come in rolls and need to be laid on top of decking — purlins won't provide sufficient support because of the flexibility of the metal.

Ribbed, corrugated and V-crimp sheets of galvanized-steel or aluminum roofing are commonly used on farm buildings and are recommended. The corrugations add rigidity to the metal. Further rigidity is possible by buying a lower gauged metal; No. 28 gauge should be ample. These sheets are available in lengths of six to thirty-two feet; they come in widths up to four feet. Therefore large areas can be covered quickly.

Buy ribbed or corrugated panels in 12-foot lengths for this shed. One sheet usually covers 24 inches after the side lap allowance. You will need four twelve-foot sheets. If you buy sheets in four-foot widths, you will need only two panels.

There are various lapping techniques for metal roofing: V-crimp, prime rib, double rib, grand rib, and corrugated, and the sheets can be made of either galvanized steel or aluminum.

Accessories

Most manufacturers sell the accessories made to fit their products, such as proper nails, trim, filler strips and sealants. Follow their instructions and use the same style and type of roofing throughout. Do not mix metals.

Should any of the panels need to be trimmed, cut the metal with tin snips. A circular or jig saw can be used with a metal cutting blade. If the sheet is to be cut lengthwise, score it with a utility knife and bend the sheet back on the scoring line.

Corrugated Roofing

Some corrugated, galvanized-steel sheets are 26 inches wide with 1 1/2-inch corrugations. Others are 27 1/2 inches wide with 2 1/2-inch corrugations, but when the sheets are lapped the usable widths will be twenty-four inches. The larger the corrugation, the stronger the panel. Even though sheets of 1 1/2-inch corrugations will have more ridges, the sheet will not be as strong as the 2 1/2-inch pattern.

The aluminum sheets come with corrugations of 1 1/4 and 2 1/2 inches.

Apply the sheets vertically, working towards the direction of the prevailing winds. Then wind, rain and snow will blow over, not under, the laps.

Align the first sheet with care or the whole roof will be out of square. The galvanized-steel sheets should be fastened at the laps with galvanized-steel ring- or screw-shank nails and lead or neoprene washers. The galvanized steel protects against rust; the washers will seal the nail holes and protect against leakage.

How To Nail

For aluminum roofing, use aluminum nails with neoprene washers under the heads.

The nails should be driven through the high part of a corrugation. Be sure they are long enough to fasten the roofing tightly to the purlins. The nails should penetrate the 2 × 4s by at least one inch; to determine the nail length, add one inch to the thickness of the corrugation (a 1 3/4- or 2-inch nail should be sufficient).

At both eaves nail every other corrugation. Nail every third corrugation on the intermediate purlins.

Do not under-drive the nails; they may work themselves loose. Do not over-drive the nails; this will compress or damage the washers and either dimple or flatten the corrugation.

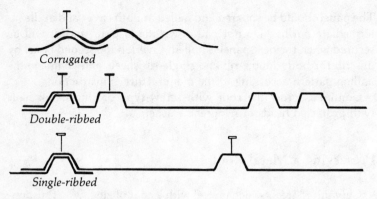

Corrugated

Double-ribbed

Single-ribbed

How to nail various types of roofing.

To prevent driving a nail that misses a purlin, align and secure the sheet both top and bottom. Mark off two-foot centers on the panel with a chalkline. Have a helper hold one end of the line over the purlin. Stretch the cord over the 2 × 4 and snap a line which will locate the center of the purlin. Do this for all the intermediate purlins.

Should you inadvertantly miss a purlin, pull out the nail and fill the hole with a sheet metal screw or rubber sealant recommended by the manufacturer. The same thing should be done if you discover an enlarged nail hole.

Ribbed Roofing

V-crimp sheets of metal roofing with two to three crimps should be laid with a side lap of one crimp. Sheets with five crimps should be laid with a side lap of two crimps. The five-crimp sheets provide a more watertight seal than sheets with only one overlap.

Ribbed roofing can be single or double ribbed. Nail the manufacturer's gable trim along the rake with roofing nails at twelve-inch intervals. The molded-rubber filler strip should be tacked to the eave. The nails which will pass through the metal roofing will secure this strip.

Start at the edge furthest from the prevailing winds to prevent rain or snow from leaking into the structure between the sheets.

The panel should be squared and nailed at both eaves and at the intermediate purlins. Do not nail down the last rib since it will be secured when the next panel is nailed. Overlap the second panel by one rib for both double-rib and single-rib sheets and complete the nailing pattern according to the manufacturer's instructions

Continue across the roof with screw-type or ring-shank nails with protected heads or neoprene washers.

Preserving a Metal Roof

Galvanized steel, which is steel with a coat of zinc, won't rust until the zinc wears off. The durability of the metal depends on this coating. The heavier the zinc, the longer the life. The gauge of the steel has nothing to do with the thickness of the zinc. To indicate a thicker coating of zinc, the metal is marked with the 2-oz. "Seal of Quality" which specifies a heavier coating of zinc on galvanized-steel sheets. Look for this "Seal of Quality" if you live in an area of extremely rigorous weather conditions or highly corrosive industrial or seashore atmosphere.

The galvanized steel should weather for at least one year before being painted; in fact the steel should give years of service before it will need painting. Although the steel can be painted immediately, weathering is desirable (but not necessary) to achieve good adhesion when the correct paint is used.

Buy zinc-rich paint and purchase only the top grade of paint — at least for the first coat. Zinc-dust paints adhere the best. Do not use aluminum paints. They will bleed because the two metals are incompatible. Two coats are better than one, but the second coat can be ordinary house or trim paint.

Don't wait too long before you paint; the best time is when the first rust begins to show. Before painting, clean the roof thoroughly. Remove loose dirt and rust spots with a stiff broom or wire brush. Remove oil or grease with a solvent and wash the entire surface with a brush and water. Check the nails. Some may have to be re-nailed.

Paint the roof in warm, dry weather (at least 40°F.). Apply the zinc-base paint with a brush, high-pressure sprayer, or long nap roller.

Aluminum doesn't need to be painted, and if the steel is coated with aluminum or aluminum-zinc, the steel can be left unpainted.

Repairs

Repairs to metal roofs are simple. Sometimes the sheets pull away at the side laps. Remove the nails and reset them to make a tighter fit. If the nails will not hold, use sheet metal screws to pull the sheets together. Drill a small hole through the two sheets at the peak of the corrugation and screw in a size 12 or 14 sheet metal screw. Drive in a new nail one inch away. Enlarged nail holes should be filled this way with extra nails added along the sides.

Leaks can be stopped with a coat of roofing cement or a drop of solder. Larger holes should be covered with a new piece of the same metal. (A fiberglass patch should be used for aluminum which cannot be soldered, and for any roof that has been coated with tar or roofing cement.) Cut a patch at least two inches larger than the hole. Snip off the corners and turn back the edges 1/2 inch. Sand the turned edge to a shine. Coat it and the corresponding roof surface with flux. Lay the patch in place; weigh it down with bricks or stones. Use an electric soldering iron and heat the edge of the patch until the solid-core solder flows freely into the joint. Work around all four sides. Wipe away the residue.

Storm Damage

If a bad storm has partially ruined the roof, remove the damaged sheets and replace them, keeping the same overlap pattern. Be careful not to damage the usable sheets when removing nails.

Remember that aluminum and galvanized steel aren't compatible. Do not make repairs with aluminum panels on a roof of galvanized steel or vice versa. The two metal have a corrosive effect on each other.

If leakage occurs along an entire side lap, the two sheets should be caulked. Butyl rubber or a caulking compound recommended by the manufacturer may be used. Loosen the side lap nails with a screwdriver. Pry up the top sheet and force the sealant between the sheets in a continuous bead. Reset the nails and caulk the nail holes carefully. If any are enlarged, fill them with sealant or sheet metal screws, and renail one inch away.

Alternate Roofing

You may object to a metal roof. It may not be in keeping with the rest of the buildings on your property or you may want to use left-over roofing materials from other projects. Wood shingles or asphalt shingles can be used, but they are unnecessary and expensive for this kind of structure.

Any roof other than a metal one will require decking and of the roofs requiring decking, roll roofing is the fastest, easiest and least expensive to lay. It is especially suitable for roofs with such a shallow slope and costs 15 percent less than asphalt shingles.

The rafters should be spaced on two-foot centers. (This will necessitate another 2 × 6 × 12.) The plywood sheathing of 4' × 8' × 1/2" exterior grade is nailed directly to the rafters. Begin at the rake (the side edge of the roof), and lay the plywood with the face grain perpendicular to the rafters. Nail the sheet in place with 6d nails spaced every six inches at the edges and every twelve inches at the rafters in between. To insure that the nails don't miss the rafters, snap chalklines along the rafters. Lay the second piece in place leaving 1/16-inch space between the two.

Protect the roof with a drip edge around the eaves and rakes. It should fit snugly. Drip edge can be cut with tin snips. Nail it down with roofing nails centered in the top surface and spaced every twelve inches.

Start laying the roofing from the rake. Cut to length plus 1/2 inch a starter strip nineteen inches wide from the selvage portion of the roll. This will leave a 1/4-inch overhang at each edge. The seventeen-inch remaining strip that has the crushed mineral surface will be used for the last course. Lay the smooth tar-coated piece in place, leaving a slight overhang on three sides. Fasten it with roofing nails spaced one-foot apart in three horizontal rows. Locate the nails about six inches apart. Use galvanized roofing nails.

Cut the next strip to length using the full width of the roll roofing. (Add 1/2-inch for the overhang.) Nail it down in two rows eight inches apart and the nails spaced every twelve inches. Lift the mineral surface of each course and coat the upper nineteen-inch portion of the previous strip with quick-setting asphalt cement to within 1/4 inch of the exposed edge. Roll the mineral surface back into place.

Each succeeding strip should overlap the previous one by nineteen inches, with seventeen inches of the mineral surface exposed at each course. The upper portion of each strip should be cemented. Use the coated half left over from the starter piece for the last strip.

After the roof has been finished, check for any loose laps and recement them.

Many people think roll roofing is unattractive. However if the job is done neatly, none of the nails or cement should show. And if the roof is almost flat yet eight feet high, it shouldn't be visible.

Enclosing the Shed

Much less air will be able to circulate throughout the wood if the storage shed is enclosed. For this reason leave as many sides open as possible. If you have bad winds, primarily from one direction, you may wish to enclose that side. From the top of the eave girder, measure down each pole 45 1/4 inches. This will give the top edge for a 2 × 6 girt. A second girt should be one foot or so from the ground.

Scrap lumber of slab wood can be used to span the distance between the girts, or plywood can be used. Scab onto the posts with scrap 2 × 4s to provide a nailing surface. A full 4 × 8 × 1/2-inch sheet of CDX plywood should be pushed up against the rafters and nailed to the 2 × 8 girder, the 2 × 6 girt, and to the nailers.

The second sheet will have to be ripped. Measure from the bottom of the plywood sheet already in place. This measurement will vary along the plywood because of variations in the terrain. Cut the second piece of plywood to the shortest dimension minus six to twelve inches. This extra space will provide for air circulation.

A less permanent solution would be a canvas tarp which could roll down to protect the pile from the prevailing winds in winter but allow the spring breezes. Polyethylene plastic of four mils could be stapled down for seasonal protection. Roll the ends around lath to prevent the plastic from tearing.

Plastic will deteriorate badly after a few months' exposure to intense sunlight. You may have to replace it every year or two.

Don't enclose the whole structure. At least one end must be left open for ease of handling wood. And air circulation is important as is the warmth of the sun which should reach the wood whenever possible.

Stacking the Wood

Wood will season much more quickly if it is stacked, with some accommodation for ventilation. If space is no problem, wood stacked criss-cross (for six months, then in a parallel fashion) will dry more rapidly. If storage is a problem or you don't relish the prospect of restacking the pile, then it can be stacked in parallel fashion in the storage shed. Remember that if stacked in long rows it will take much longer to dry and the lower layers may rot before they season.

When stacking the wood, some provision must be made to keep it off the ground. Stringers can be laid down approximately a foot apart and the wood stacked on these, or wood pallets can be used if they are available locally.

Criss-cross the end logs as you build up on the pile and tilt these logs slightly towards the center of the pile. You may even want to pile a set of splits criss-cross in the center of the pile for greater stability. End braces shouldn't be necessary but can be used if you have difficulty stacking wood, or if the pile collapses at either end.

The piles should go the long way of the shed, and with space between the rows for ventilation.

Since dry wood has more heat value than green, keep close track of which wood you've stacked where. Use the first-cut wood first, particularly since wood can be stored too long. Decay will markedly reduce the wood's heat value. Unsplit wood with its bark still on will become moist and punky inside because the bark has prevented water loss. Birch will rot quickly; hickory, beech and hard maple are susceptible to rot and fungi; cedar, oak, black locust and black walnut are most durable.

You may wish to separate hardwoods and softwoods. The softwoods ignite more easily and burn more rapidly than the hardwoods. Therefore they are ideal for kindling.

In one portion of the shed build a bin for kindling, twigs, birch bark, shavings, pine cones, corn cobs, dried citrus peels, lath, scraps from lumberyards, or whatever else you may collect during the year for tinder. It can also be a receptacle for wood chips found around the chopping block.

How to Check for Green Wood

Even with a storage shed, you may run out of wood, and have to use wood cut this year. Since some woods may be greener than others, it will be useful to know how to identify green wood — just split a piece. The core will look wet and shiny; dry wood looks dull and the saw marks are much less pronounced.

Green wood is almost twice as heavy as seasoned wood and will make a dull thud when two sticks are hit together. Green wood is hard to handle, hard to light and burns slowly. Much of its heat value is lost in heating, then evaporating, the excess moisture.

As wood dries, the moisture evaporates naturally and the wood begins to shrink. (Wood even when air dry is still 20-25 percent moisture.) Since wood dries unevenly, cracking and checking of the wood occurs. Dried wood can be recognized by the weathered ends and by the cracks which will radiate like spokes out from the heartwood.

Green wood can be used to dampen an excessively hot fire or used at night to help hold a fire overnight. It tends to smoke more than dry wood and therefore increases creosote deposits and soot. If you must use green wood, use it during the day when the fire is the hottest.

To be more scientific about the process, you can weigh a split just after it has been cut; then weigh it again in nine months and figure the weight loss. Oven-drying will also give you an indication of moisture loss. Weigh the wood, then leave it in the oven at a low setting. After a few hours, you should know how much by weight the wood has lost.

Seasoned Wood

In order to avoid burning green wood, it is important to establish a wood storage routine which hastens the drying of your wood fuel supply. A pole-built shed is a simple, practical method of insuring you get the full heat potential from the wood. In addition, you will be increasing the burning efficiency of your stove while decreasing the possibility of chimney fires.

Approximate Weights and Heat Values for Different Woods

	Weight/cord		Available heat Million BTU	
	Green	Air dry	Green	Air dry
Ash	3840	3440	16.5	20.0
Aspen	3440	2160	10.3	12.5
Beech, American	4320	3760	17.3	21.8
Birch, yellow	4560	3680	17.3	21.3
Elm, American	4320	2900	14.3	17.2
Hickory, shagbark	5040	4240	20.7	24.6
Maple, red	4000	3200	15.0	18.6
Maple, sugar	4480	3680	18.4	21.3
Oak, red	5120	3680	17.9	21.3
Oak, white	5040	3920	19.2	22.7
Pine, eastern white	2880	2080	12.1	13.3